香港國際詩歌之夜 *2013*
INTERNATIONAL POETRY NIGHTS IN HONG KONG

編輯 Editors

北島 Bei Dao

陳嘉恩 Shelby K. Y. Chan

方梓勳 Gilbert C. F. Fong

柯夏智 Lucas Klein

馬德松 Christopher Mattison

楊君磊
Jeffrey Yang

目錄 Contents

1 Five Poems from *An Aquarium* (2008)

Eel

Eels are slimy creatures.
But never lie. If they sense
the slightest pretence, they'll
bite off your finger. Carefully
study the hands of politicians.

Kelp

How easy it is to lose oneself
in a kelp forest. Between
canopy leaves, sunlight filters thru
the water surface; nutrients
bring life where there'd other-
wise be barren sea; a vast eco-
system breathes. Each
being being
being's link.

Lobster

Impossible to doubt
the lobster's sorrow. Like a
wordless shudder pain
passes between us. Empty
shell of the subject
inscribes pain's grammar.
Sorrow and pain inflect
one another. Alive
the lobster's been drowned
in fresh water, packed in
sawdust, packed in ice, packed
in polystyrene, packed upright
in gel ice, boiled in brine, slow
frozen, knifed, banded, pegged,
electrocuted, and most recently
hydrostatic pressurized. The U.S.
still absorbs most
of the world's lobsters. War
and protectionism:
two causes of starvation.

Orca

The Chinese call orcas "tiger
whales"; Pliny likened them to
warships; a *Yuukara* song of the Saru
Ainu goes, "Killer whale, god of the ocean,
please bring more than one and a half
whales every year. Then, I'll
be pleased to give my sweet daughter as a bride."
High on the Nazca Desert is the orca's image.
The Tlingit are also matrilineal. Taxonomically
the orca's a whale within a dolphin within a whale.
And never known to harm a human
unless forced to do chlorinated circus
tricks, in which case they die young.

Xiangjun

Follow the twelfth guideway thru
the Middle Mountains to the realm
of the Nine Rivers where Xiao
flows into Xiang and tear-stained
bamboo grows. In this place four
thousand years ago the Xiangjun
drowned themselves: two daughters
of Yao, wives of Shun. Not even
geese can bear their water-spirit
sorrow. Tang poet Qian Qi:

Why rashly turn back   once at the Xiao-Xiang
Blue-green waters   bright sand   moss on both banks
Twenty-five strings plucked on moonlit nights   an
unbearable   pure melancholy   so they take flight

《水族館》五首

鰻魚

鰻魚是滑手膩心的生物。
但從不說謊。如果它們察覺出
你有半點兒作假,它們也會
咬掉你的手指。仔細
看看那些政客的手。

海帶

太容易迷失在
海帶的叢林。被水面過濾的陽光
灑入蓬蓬葉片。養料
帶來生命否則就是
荒涼的大海。一個龐大的
生態系統呼吸著。每一條
命都連著另一條
命。

龍蝦

不可能懷疑
龍蝦的悲哀。像一道
無言的戰慄之痛
從我們中間穿過。身
的空殼刻寫著
疼痛的語法。
悲哀與疼痛相互
映照。龍蝦活著
既已被投入
清水,封入
鋸末,封入冰,封入
聚苯乙烯,被豎著
封入膠冰,煮於鹽水,
緩凍,刀切,捆紮,固定,
電死,還有最新近的
靜水壓力法。美國
仍在吞噬著
全球大多數龍蝦。戰爭
與貿易保護主義:
導致饑餓的兩大原因。

逆戟鯨

逆戟鯨，中國人稱作「虎
鯨」；普林尼將它們比作
戰艦；沙流川的阿伊努人在一首
Yunkara 歌中唱到：「屠手鯨，大洋之神，
拜託每年帶來大鯨一頭半，
或更多更好。如此，我會
樂得獻出我甜美的女兒做你的新娘。」
逆戟鯨的形象甚至深入納茲卡沙漠。
特林吉特人還是母系社會。分類學上
逆戟鯨既算海豚又屬鯨。
從沒聽說它們傷過人
除非被迫戲耍於馬戲團的
加氯消毒水池，這使它們早早死去。

湘君

循第十二列山系穿越

中央群山抵達

九條江水之域，這裏

瀟湘匯流，斑竹

生長。四千年前

湘君在此沉溺：是堯

之二女，舜之二妃。這水之靈

即使大雁也難忍

其悲。唐人錢起詩云：

瀟湘何事等閒回

水碧沙明兩岸苔

二十五弦彈夜月

不勝清怨卻飛來

（西川、尹冉旭譯）

譯註：

1. 「循第十二列山系穿越中央群山抵達九條江水之域」：
   原文the twelfth guideway 所言，應源自《山海經・卷
   五・中山經》。後文「堯之二女」事亦見此卷。《山海
   經》原文：「中次十二經洞庭山之首」云云，袁珂《山
   海經全譯》（貴州人民出版社，1991）作「中央第十二
   列山系洞庭山的開頭一座山……」。譯文據此而出。
2. 原詩中所引錢起詩英譯文不知何人所為，英譯文行中有
   空格。

2 Three Poems from *Lyric Suite*

Trees turned to branches
yellow leaves all around

the city, rain-
fall

Elder one leaving

the corner for
the road

            behind

memory
    * * *

west of rest is sleep
east, dream
where waters meet
north, emptiness,
south, wakefulness,
and out, rising up

to the stars, peace

* * *

On West Lake she boats
childhood summer wind
endless
      radiance
Fold upon fold
of lotus-
bloom water
      circling Sun

《抒情組曲》三首

樹木探出樹杈
黃葉滿身

城市，雨
落下

老人離開

道路的
拐角

　　在記憶的

後面
　　　＊ ＊ ＊
休憩，西邊是睡眠
東邊是夢境
水流交匯處
北方，空空，
南方，清醒，

靈魂出竅，升向
星宿，寧靜
    * * *
她泛舟於西湖
童年夏日的風兒
無盡
    波光
蓮花
疊曳的
水面
    環抱著太陽

（西川、夏天眉譯）

3 Four Poems from *Yennecott*

Out the screen door
to flowers, fresh cut grass
a low umbrella'd table
two Adirondack chairs
between bushes step
down to a thin stretch of
sand high tide hides, leaves
behind stones, shells, sea

      * * *

Urubamba flow below Vilcapampa
city of stairways in the clouds

The way Castillo's quill trembled
before the undreamed
that was already dreamed

ancient memory

Gandharva realm, keyed
stone carved, angled
vicuña rug, their love

for sun
terrace tillage
harmony of water-
lightness tied
to intihuatana
mirror of bronze

Sun's reflection, echo
of Tiahuanaco

ruins Mayta Capac studied
Pachacutec curved walls

ashlar room window heights
milder than Cusco
hidden by mountains
mist home temple

hidden from conquest

when the merciful conquerors

became the conquered

And the place abandoned imagination
        * * *
bark walls bullrush mats
and the living place: open sky
        * * *
Walked the shore of shells
Walked the dock, the glass
Peninsula, the broken pier
Walked the macadam to
Grassy field, walked the path
Thru the trees towering to sand
Walked the morning dove's nest
In shade and leaves
Walked the templum
Of elfin gold, of orpiment crystals
Tempered with wine
Walked the brickhouse and outhouse
Walked the water back to where
I began

(tho I could see no semblance of a beginning)
And what the walk revealed
Along the sea's margin
Along the rimrock
Of the island
After so many centuries
Of marsh-tides and moonstones
Of or and ore (before oar)
Was an experience of walking
Irony replaced with nothingness
Immensity and transience
The unsaid
Thoughts flowing round my heart
And the rays like a shepherd's fire
Shadowing the vanishing-line

《耶內考特》四首

出紗門
見花朵、新剪的草
遮陽傘下低矮的桌子
兩把阿迪朗達克條板木椅
兩旁是灌木，走
下去是一小片
沙灘，大潮隱伏，岩石
擋住樹葉，貝殼，海洋
　　　　　* * *
維卡潘巴，雲中的階梯之城
城下奔流著烏魯班巴河

卡斯提略羽毛管顫動的樣子
在未入夢之前
早已被夢見過

遠古的記憶

雅樂之神乾闥婆的國度，起興的
石頭被刻寫，卷角的
小羊駝毛毯，它們

對太陽的愛
梯田
拴日石拴住的
澹澹之水的
和諧
青銅鏡

太陽的反光
蒂亞瓦納科廢墟的回聲

印加王梅塔·卡佩克研究過
潘查庫泰克彎曲的城牆

方石屋的窗高
沒有庫斯科城那般過分
躲隱於群山
這霧之家這廟宇

躲開了征服

當仁慈的征服者

變成被征服者

此地放棄了想像
　　　　＊　＊　＊
樹皮牆蘆葦墊
生存之地：廣闊的天空
　　　　＊　＊　＊
走過貝殼的海岸
走過碼頭，玻璃的
半島，失修的防波堤
從碎石柏油路走向
草野，走小徑
穿過樹叢它們高聳向沙灘
走過蔭遮葉護的
清晨的鴿巢
走過混合著酒氣的
雌黃晶體那小精靈黃金的
廟堂
走過磚房和單體小屋
走到水邊重返我的
開始之處

（儘管我看不出任何開始的跡象）

走，沿著大海的邊緣

沿著島嶼的懸崖

在太多的沼澤潮浸和月光石的

世紀之後

在（無槳時代）太多原礦和不確定的

世紀之後

走揭示出走的經驗

取代反諷的是空白

無限和短暫

這些默然的思緒

繞心環流

其光亮有如牧人的篝火

模糊了讓事物消失的天際線

（西川、夏天眉譯）

譯註：

在印度神話中，乾闥婆(Gandharva)原來是一群半神半人的
天上樂師，是帝釋天屬下職司雅樂的天神。乾闥婆亦為東方
持國天的眷屬，為守護東方之神，同時也是觀音二十八部眾
之一。

4 Elegy for Ling

spirit consumed by fire
shaman warps to pig's head
rain above open mouths
doorway
between shaman and rainfall

ling heart-
tone
of the temple gate
of the zero-moon

echo of jade brilliance
red phosphorous spirit
          spirit
of being un-
making *ling*

soul dim light flit-
ting
eaves splitting maborosi light will-
o'-the-wisp

drawing her nearer

across
what distances
                  darknesses

ling

beyond the waste mountains
water stream-
ing stones
        that
sound of
water against stones
of jade pendants
of bells
of antelope horns among branches
of damask
of feathers of
the creaking wheel
ling

unrecognizable behind the lattice
pages and pages float-
ing down

scales
scars tearing apart, heart
sliver of light ice prison

to the measured position

of the cracking entablature
at the architrave's cusp
crumbling beneath her

ling
looking down

on the ruined city of her birth
facing

the unraveling

the expanding the contracting
the pull of the end

that night before the wedding
before her arrival

where were you ling
sewing the wedding dress

sewing the seconds

her little brother before her

the boy who jumped thru the atrium
the boy with the gun, the boy who drowned

old men sorting thru rubble, brick by brick
rebuilding the ancient walls
while the ring roads expand
while the machinery explodes
the celebrity architects multiply

ignorant of the original design

coal in the lungs sand in the lungs
carbon monoxide poly-
chlorinated biphenyl red
dust in the lungs

the hanged woman's house sold
her belongings sold windows barred
tree cursed

the man on his bicycle hit by a train

it was pouring rain

on the forest on the thorptops

that night before the wedding
before her arrival

ancient observatory

wrapped between highways
between hotels and satellite dishes
billboards and metal cranes
   at the intersection
daoists buddhists muslims
weighing the heavens, watching
with bronze instruments on a roof of stone
before the jesuits, before verbiest's refitting
his *ruder muse*, before stumpf's melting of the yuan
3300 years ago a nova guest star recorded on an oracle
 bone
now gaseous haze for sky
electricity spinning arenaceous air
drowning perception
of the forged inventions
armillary spheres
red road equatorial *yellow road* ecliptic
quadrant sextant celestial globe
polar axis spins positioning the stars
dragon theodolite azimuth theodolite

at theta at teth at sun at death

like drowning in open ocean, I.C. wrote

the map was there, her laugh is there
alone with the signs

the patterns the biochemicals
the codons the proteins
translating un-
folding

the final despair of the final decision
eyes clear eyes bright
to the received translation

ling
cipher spirit-source

ling
mystical deer mystical fish

anteater wagtail dace

ling
Libellulidae winging water
      chestnut
      fall-
ing
          rain

thru the threshold
of the mind

of the wine
of the sill
of the thin stone port-
hole boat bottle with handle
tilling channel accumulating
ice

ling
tomb plume mound coffin

yin of the *wu*-shaman
Quercus on Sumeru

lonely lake wound-
ing light

traversing the lintel

for us left
the looking forward looking back
at the bridge at the river

without reconciliation without expiation
sound breaking clear

ing

eyes of turquoise and coral
cannot see

motherless children
love's innocence

children

on the stairs

靈之輓歌

幽靈被火焰吞噬
巫師向豬頭弓腰
雨落入張開的嘴
門道
在巫師和雨水之間

靈
寺廟山門
和零月亮的
心音

是玉之光韻的回聲
是恢復
靈
的紅色磷火的幽靈
　　　幽靈

靈魂忽明忽暗地
掠過
屋簷撕開幻之光那一縷
心願

讓她靠近

穿越
所謂距離
　　　　黑暗

靈

在荒山之上
溪水沖刷
亂石
　　發出
流水漱石的
聲音
冷冷玉墜兒的聲音
打鐘的聲音
枝杈間羚羊角號的聲音
錦緞的聲音
吱嘎作響的輪子上
羽毛的聲音
靈

在窗格後面模糊不清
一頁頁飄
零而去的

尺度
扯開的傷疤，光閃閃的
冰窟裏心的碎塊兒

下落到測算好的位置

柱頂過梁的尖頭上
皸裂的木楣
損毀在她的下面

靈
俯視

她出生城市的廢墟
面對

崩散

擴展與收縮
被拖來的終結

那一夜在婚禮之前
在她到來之前

你在哪裏　靈
縫著嫁衣

縫著分秒

她的小弟在她面前

那蹦跳著穿過天井的男孩
持槍的男孩，溺死的男孩

老者當他們收拾瓦礫，一磚磚
重建古代的城牆
當環路擴展
當機械轟響
明星建築師對原初規劃

暴長出無知

肺裏的煤塵肺裏的沙塵
肺裏的
一氧化碳
多氯聯苯紅塵

曾有女人上吊的房屋被賣掉
她的東西被賣掉窗戶被封上
樹被詛咒

騎自行車的男人被火車撞倒

大雨傾盆而下

落在樹林上落在鄉鎮的頭頂上

那一夜在婚禮之前
在她到來之前

古觀象臺

被圍裹在高架橋和道路中間
賓館和衛星天線鍋中間
看板和起重機中間
　　　　在叉路口的一角
道教徒佛教徒穆斯林
稱著天堂的重量，在石臺上
憑青銅儀器觀測
在耶穌會傳教士之前，在南懷仁改進
他笨拙的繆斯之前，在紀理安熔化他的元代之前
3,300 年前一顆新–客星被燒錄於甲骨
現在空中霧靄繚繞
電流旋轉於多沙的空氣
淹沒了
著力發明的念頭
各圈狀儀器
所標「赤道」即equator「黃道」即ecliptic
象限儀六分儀天球儀
極軸旋轉指向群星
龍經緯儀地平經緯儀

指著第八個希臘字母第九個希伯來字母指著太陽指

著死亡

就像淹沒於汪洋大海，I.C.寫道

地圖曾在那兒，她的笑聲
與那些標誌單獨在一起

生化模型
基碼蛋白質
譯解
打開

最後決定的最後絕望
眼神清澈又明亮
面對公認的譯解

靈
可以忽略不計的幽靈之源

靈
奧秘之鹿奧秘之魚

奧秘之食蟻獸鵲鴿鳥和鯑魚

靈
蜻蛉點水
　　　栗子
　　　落
下
　　　　　　雨

落入心靈的
門檻

酒瓶口
窗臺
舷窗窄小的
石舫帶把的瓶子
積冰的
灌渠

靈
墳墓上的羽毛土堆中的棺材

巫師的　陰
須彌山上的櫟樹

孤獨的湖面上
刺目的光

打門楣下走過

剩給我們的是
左看看右看看
看著橋樑與河水

沒有和解沒有補償
清晰的碎裂之

聲

綠松石與珊瑚的眼睛
看不見

沒媽的孩子

愛的天真

　　孩子

在樓梯上

（西川、華佳譯）

譯註：

1. 南懷仁(Ferdinand Verbiest)，字敦伯，又字勳卿，比利
時人，1623 年生於布魯塞爾，1641 年入耶穌會，1658
年來華。他是康熙皇帝的科學啟蒙老師，精通天文曆
法、擅長鑄炮，是當時國家天文臺（欽天監）業務上的
最高負責人，官至工部侍郎，正二品。1688 年在北京逝
世，諡勤敏。著有《康熙永年曆法》、《坤輿圖說》、
《西方要記》等。詩中所説「笨拙的繆斯」原文 ruder
muse，指南懷仁於 1672 年重建北京觀象臺時，棄置元
代遺存的舊儀器，並在他於 1687 年出版的《歐洲天文
學》(*Astronomia Europaea*) 一書中有此一説。事見1975
年科學出版社出版、英國李約瑟著，《中國科學技術史》
中譯本（集體翻譯），第四卷，天學第二分冊，頁497
(Joseph Needham: *Science & Civilisation in China*,
Vol. III, pp. 379–380, Cambridge University Press)。

2. 康熙54年（1715年），耶穌會神父紀理安(B. K. Stumpf)
   為製作地平經緯儀而熔化了元代王恂、郭守敬創制的仰
   儀、簡儀等數種儀器。李約瑟在其《中國科學技術史》
   天學卷的一個註腳中提到此事。另見曹增友著，《傳教
   士與中國科學》（宗教文化出版社，1999），頁50。
3. 「新－客星」，原文nova guest star。據李約瑟《中國科
   學技術史》天學卷，在甲骨學家、古史學家董作賓所研
   究的殷墟甲骨中，有一片上面提到新星（該甲骨原文「新
   大星」）。為人類遺留至今的最古新星記錄。但「新星」
   的說法到漢代中葉被「客星」二字所取代。國際天文學
   界稱新星為novae。

楊君磊於1974年生於美國加州埃斯孔迪多，著有詩集《漸褪的線》(2011) 及《水族館》（「國際筆會喬依斯・奧斯特韋爾詩歌獎」得獎作品，2008）；兩部作品皆由Graywolf Press出版。過去13年他於出版社New Directions擔任編輯，曾編纂詩選《沉痛時光：悲慟詩句及鳥》及《野獸及大海：自然界詩選》。楊君磊的譯作包括劉曉波的《念念六四》、蘇軾的《東坡》、唐宋詩集及《千家詩》，他又與譯者娜塔莎・威默合編世界文學年度選集《二線：一些美麗符號》。楊氏亦為《紐約書評》編輯，協助創辦《紐約書評》詩人系列。

（吳詠雯譯）

Jeffrey Yang was born in 1974 in Escondido, California. He is the author of the poetry books *Vanishing-Line* (2011) and *An Aquarium* (2008, winner of the PEN/Joyce Osterweil Award), both published by Graywolf Press. For the past thirteen years Yang has worked as an editor at New Directions, and has edited two anthologies for the publishing house—*Time of Grief: Mourning Poems* and *Birds, Beasts, and Seas: Nature Poems from New Directions*. He is the translator of Liu Xiaobo's *June Fourth Elegies*, Su Shi's *East Slope*, and the collection of Tang and Song poems, the *Qian Jia Shi*, titled *Rhythm 226*. With the translator Natasha Wimmer, he edited the annual anthology of world literature, *Two Lines: Some Kind of Beautiful Signal*. Yang also works as an editor for New York Review Books, where he helped start their new NYRB/Poets series.

出版 Publisher
香港中文大學出版社 The Chinese University Press

封面影像 Cover Image
北島 Bei Dao

出版日期 Date of Publication
二零一三年十一月 November 2013

國際書號 ISBN
978-962-996-623-2

香港國際詩歌之夜 2013 International Poetry Nights in Hong Kong 2013
主辦單位 Organizers
香港中文大學文學院 Faculty of Arts, The Chinese University of Hong Kong
香港浸會大學文學院 Faculty of Arts, Hong Kong Baptist University
香港科技大學人文社會科學學院 School of Humanities and Social Science,
The Hong Kong University of Science and Technology

合作夥伴 In Partnership With
英國文化協會 British Council

協辦單位 Co-organizers
時刻文化 Moment Communications
香港中文大學出版社 The Chinese University Press

贊助 Sponsors
香港兆基創意書院 HKICC Lee Shau Kee School of Creativity
中國會 The China Club
周凱旋基金會 Chau Hoi Shuen Foundation

Printed in Hong Kong